Ralph Baumgartner

ODDS & ENDS

'AN IMAGINED LIFE'

RoseDog Books

PITTSBURGH, PENNSYLVANIA 15238

RoseDog Books
585 Alpha Drive
Suite 103
Pittsburgh, PA 15238
Visit our website at *www.rosedogbookstore.com*

ISBN: 979-8-88527-533-0
eISBN: 979-8-88527-583-5

ODDS & ENDS

'AN IMAGINED LIFE'

CONTENTS

TOO GOOD A DAY

Walking down the mountain side,

I saw a man who did not hide,

And when I confronted him, he cried.

He told me how throughout his years,

He'd witnessed the shedding of many tears,

And nature's songs no one would hear.

He told me stories of hell in war,

How his dad was killed in a country store,

And then continued to tell me more.

I couldn't take it so I walked away,

It was just too good a day.

THE WORLD I LOVED

I remember,

This long winding road,

That lost itself into the forest,

And a gentle easy stream,

That would break the road at lengths.

I remember,

Walking this road for hours,

And fishing in the stream,

During long sunny summers,

And crispy winter days.

I remember,

How the birds would sing in the morning,

How the clouds would dot the sky,

How beautiful was the sunsets,

And how each day brought new hope.

I also remember,

Along with the good came the bad,

Friends and family would pass away,

And progress inched its way,

Into the arms of mother nature.

But they shall never steal my memories,

And they shall never cloud my dreams,

Until our good Lord cancels the show.

TAKE NOTE

Take note Sir Leon-
The mountains, jagged as they are,
Salute the sun, caress the stars,
The trees tremendous, tall and green,
Protect the meadows, shade the stream.

Note also that the scope of things,
Appears to fight against itself,
Like giant dinosaur on wing.
For what is large is large,
And what is small is small,
And together makes an odd setting.

But take note Sir Leon-
There is great calm in the air,
As if there never was a care.
And check the fence along the road,
Just what the devil does it serve,
Is it my prison or is it theirs?

HAVING LIVED

I have lived,
and with each turning of a page,
a time is lost,
and a time begun,
in ceaseless repetition.

I have lived,
and with the passage of time,
has come a knowing,
as well as a feeling,
of what is right and wrong.

I have lived,
and as age besieges me,
I notice the young,
starting as I had done,
learning from each turning of a page.

I have lived,
and have not regretted living,
 and though death awaits me,
I do not await death,
but assault it with life.

OUR MASKS

I wear a mask
You cannot see me
And I cannot see me.

You wear a mask
I cannot see you
And you cannot see you.

We wear mask
And no one knows
Who we are.

We hide behind illusion
Lost within confusion
And are never fully aware
Of who is really there.

THE MAD MACHINES OF MAIN STREET

The mad machines of main street,

Have eyes that glow and rubber feet,

With constant purr and roaring,

Down main street they'll go soaring.

The time is still too early yet,

And no confusion will be met,

Till later in the evening when,

The mad and wild event begins.

Kids and young adults come out,

And drive and drive and drive about,

The mad machines of main street turning,

Ever into a constant yearning.

They come alive and haunt the night,

With eyes that glow and rubber feet,

They amass and swarm until it's right,

To head for home, to bed, to sleep.

For now the ghostly streets are bare,

Of the mad machines main street affair.

GONE TO THE GRAVEYARD

Who are these people

Lying here

In dusty homes

From yester-year?

What are their names

Where did they go

Are they anyone

That you would know?

Who are these people

Cold and dead

Gone and forgotten

In their dusty beds?

Who-can recall

A name, a face

Of such a one

In such a place?

EATING FLIES

I asked her if she thought

If love was all for naught

And if marriage was out dated

And when she finally stated

That it was, I was surprised

And with mouth dropped open wide

swallowed all the flies.

ONE OF THESE DAYS

One of these days

I'll get lost in my head

Starve on my knowledge

And then I'll be dead.

LENT

After money and time

Had all been spent

I guess she gave me

Up for lent.

LEFT AND RIGHT WING

A black dot to start

Moving at first slowly

And then with a sudden burst

Wings flapping in earnest

It swoops upon its prey;

The hawk swoops toward the east

First the left wing

Then the right wing

Propelling it toward doom.

A white dot to start

Moving at first slowly

And then with sudden speed

And a gentle sureness

It swoops upon its prey;

The dove swoops toward the west

First the left wing

Then the right wing

Propels it toward doom.

The dove and hawk pass

Knocking feathers from each other,

But their prey

Are just as dead.

A THOUSAND YEARS

The earth shall wobble, spin, and tilt,

And fill our laps up to the hilt,

With glaciers that shall dig and bite,

And drive us south with all its might.

CRITICAL REACTION

It was a critical reaction
These two opposing forces
Could have exploded
Destroying each other
Spreading their dying memories
Into the dark abyss.

But the-critical reaction
Seemingly instantaneous
Was to join forces together
And fusing into one mass
Went darting off into space
On a trajectory all Its own.

SKIING COLORADO

Together we went soaring

Down the mountains, roaring

With a silence that could kill,

And laughing at ourselves against our will.

FOR STEINBECK

One rock tumbles down

And hitting bottom stops,

While the world goes unchanged.

One rock tumbles down,

And gathers thousands for the trip,

They shake the world to make it change.

HERE WE GO

Here we go along the way.

Here we go along the way.

Don't get in your neighbors way.

And count the seconds that you stay.

Off we go now, off we go.

Through the rain and through the snow.

Through the winds of time that blow.

Off we go now, off we go.

Can't you feel it slip away.

All your dreams and yesterdays.

All the dues you had to pay.

All the objects in your way.

Off we go now, on our way.

Off we go now, off we go.

REQUIEM FOR THE DAY

Technology was the maxim,

A tedious chore for most.

But a formidable plot was enacted,

And the proud men did boast.

There were forged many trite laws,

For personal gain they had no flaws.

The criterion used as base,

Was well adjusted to save face.

With drawn out wars procured,

Bringing the procession to death in herds.

The massive waste of man power,

Was replaced by advanced machine power.

The basic family brought to extinction.

The basic madmen grew in distinction.

Pollution laws were all abolished,

By speeches long and polished.

Now hear the requiem for the day,

All known as man be on your way.

This earth no longer is your home,

You are banished and alone.

CUBA

He is so happy, hear him cheer.

His gladness ringing in his ear.

It's his turn, he thinks, for hope.

To Cuba he's hijacked some ones boat.

THE WOODS THAT CALL

Oh, the woods, so dark inviting.

Oh, the forest, free and easy.

Invites the whippoorwill to sing.

Invites my soul to spend the spring.

Oh, the woods, so dark and deep.

Oh, the forest walls so steep.

Invites me to be lost forever.

Invite me not, I must refuse.

Oh, the woods, so dark inviting.

Oh, the forest, free and easy.

Invite me now, but not forever.

For I have many things to do.

For I have important things to do.

DAYS OF DOOM

The populace with empty hearts,
Search the souls of empty men.
The empty men in seats of glory,
Handing out their foolish laws.
Laws that cover up their falsehoods,
And keep the people unaware.

The people cry with empty hands,
To heartless leaders in endless lands.
The leaders wander as we wonder,
Standing back they go asunder.
People fighting for their lives.
Soon these leaders all will fall.

Lonely now, the people stray,
Through the nation, through the day.
Rebels once, they challenged leaders,
Went to far, and lost design.
So with a rumble, society crumbled,
And left them all their fate to pay.

www.ingramcontent.com/pod-product-compliance
Lightning Source LLC
Chambersburg PA
CBHW060949130726
48001CB00003B/1131